Tab the cat

Story written by Gill Munton
Illustrated by Tim Archbold

Speed Sounds

Consonants *Ask children to say the sounds.*

f	l	m	n	r	s	v	z	**sh**	**th**	ng
ff	**ll**		nn	**rr**	ss	ve	zz			**nk**
	le		kn				s			

b	c	d	g	h	j	p	qu	t	w	x	y	ch
bb	k	dd	gg			pp		tt	wh			tch
	ck											

Each box contains one sound but sometimes more than one grapheme.
*Focus graphemes for this story are **circled**.*

Vowels

Ask children to say the sounds in and out of order.

a	e	i	o	u	ay	ee	igh	ow
	ea					y		
at	hen	in	on	up	day	see	high	blow

oo	oo	ar	or	air	ir	ou	oy
zoo	look	car	for	fair	whirl	shout	boy

Story Green Words

Meg   Tab   rat   tank   stick   dull   nip

Ask children to say the syllables and then read the whole word.

stick in|sect   pa|rrot

Red Words

Ask children to practise reading the words across the rows, down the columns and in and out of order clearly and quickly.

want	you	call	we
be	no	her	are
the	said	your	go
he	I've	all	said

Tab the cat

Mum and Meg are in the pet shop.

9

"I will call her Tab.
Tab the cat."

Questions to talk about

Ask children to TTYP for each question using 'Fastest finger' (FF) or 'Have a think' (HaT).

p.8 (FF) What pet does Meg ask for first?

p.11 (FF) What does Meg's mum say when Meg asks for a parrot?

p.12 (HaT) Why do you think Mum does not mind having a cat?

p.13 (FF) What does Meg's mum say when Meg asks for a cat?